# Search THE SCRIPTURES

## Biblical Activity Book

### SHIRLEY D. GARRETT

WESTBOW
PRESS®
A DIVISION OF THOMAS NELSON
& ZONDERVAN

WestBow Press books may be ordered through booksellers or by contacting:

WestBow Press
A Division of Thomas Nelson & Zondervan
1663 Liberty Drive
Bloomington, IN 47403
www.westbowpress.com
844-714-3454

Scripture taken from the King James Version of the Bible.

ISBN: 978-1-6642-4454-2 (sc)
ISBN: 978-1-6642-4456-6 (hc)
ISBN: 978-1-6642-4455-9 (e)

Library of Congress Control Number: 2021918565

Print information available on the last page.

WestBow Press rev. date: 09/27/2021

# CONTENTS

# PREFACE

On Easter Sunday in 1979, a family member invited me to church, where I was introduced to Jesus Christ. I felt an inexplicable feeling of love I had never experienced before. My life hasn't been the same since. I began searching the scriptures, learning as much as I could about the word of God. I learned that God loves me and that he has a wonderful plan for my life.

In 1984, God inspired me to write a biblical activity book titled *Search the Scriptures*. It became an exciting tool for studying the word of God. I worked on the manuscript for several years before answering the call to ministry. After many years in the ministry, I came across my folder and decided to complete what I'd started many years ago.

In the Bible—God's book of wisdom—we learn how to reconnect with the God who created and loves us. It starts at the beginning and teaches us the power God has to speak life into existence. It ends with the promise of eternal life. The Bible, also known as the Holy Scriptures, is by far my favorite book to read. It brings us into fellowship with God our Father. It teaches us his plan for humanity and his instructions for a life separated from sin.

> But ye shall receive power, after that the Holy Ghost is come upon you: and ye shall be witness unto me both in Jerusalem, and in all Judaea, and

in Samaria, and unto the uttermost part of the Earth. (Acts 1:8)

Through prayer, he gives us wisdom, knowledge, and understanding of his word. The birth, life, death, and resurrection of his son Jesus Christ gave us the right to eternal life. The fear of the LORD is the beginning of wisdom: and the knowledge of the holy is understanding. (Proverbs 9:10)

The Bible is an amazing book. Reading it takes me into the presence of God. It has blessed me in my life and ministry. I hope it will bless you as well.

Shirley D. Garrett

# ACKNOWLEDGMENTS

I thank God for choosing me to write this book.

Thanks to my family, friends, and church members for all their support and for allowing me to use each of them to test run this book. I could not have done it without God or you.

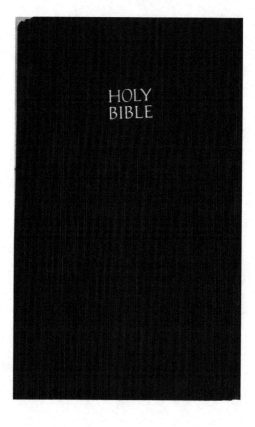

# INTRODUCTION

In this book, you will find many activities that will enhance your biblical knowledge. There are Bible-based questions, fill-in-the-blank scriptures, match games, true-and-false questions, and word search puzzles. It includes blank pages to write your notes and other information you may find during your search. Studying the word of God can be exciting, challenging, and even entertaining!

Whether you are someone who has been studying the Bible for years or you are a new learner, this book will become your favorite study tool. You will not want to put it down. Use it to enhance your Bible knowledge or to play trivia with family, friends, and church groups. This book is a fun and educational way to learn the word of God.

The answers are located in the back of the book.

# SEARCH THE SCRIPTURES

Give answer and scripture

1. What did Jacob name the place where he wrestled with the angel (God)?
   Answer:
   Scripture:

2. Who almost lost his life bringing money to Paul in prison in Rome?
   Answer:
   Scripture:

3. To which tribe of Israel did Paul belong?
   Answer:
   Scripture:

4. Who died during childbirth after praying for a second son?
   Answer:
   Scripture:

5. When the anger of the Lord was hot against Israel, to which king did he sell them?
   Answer:
   Scripture:

6. In whose house did the Ark of God remain for three months?

Answer:

Scripture:

7. Which book from the New Testament mentions the second coming of Christ in every chapter?
Answer:

Scripture:

8. Who used sorcery to bewitch the people of Samaria, but after hearing Philip preach Christ was baptized, he continued with Philip?
Answer:

Scripture:

9. At whose house did the gentiles first receive the Holy Ghost and speak with tongues that magnified God?
Answer:

Scripture:

10. Which apostle died in exile and was the only apostle not to suffer martyrdom?
Answer:

Scripture:

11. In which city did God slaughter 50,070 men because they looked into the Ark of the Covenant?
Answer:

Scripture:

12. For which of David's actions did God cause a plague on Israel?
Answer:
Scripture:

13. What animal killed forty-two children who ridiculed the bald head of the prophet Elisha?
Answer:
Scripture:

14. How did God designate those who would be spared in the Jerusalem massacre prophesied by Ezekiel?
Answer:
Scripture:

15. What request did Jephthah's daughter make before allowing herself to be sacrificed?
Answer:
Scripture:

16. What prominent individual was the first to be cremated in the Bible?
Answer:
Scripture:

17. How many cities in Canaan were given to the Levites, excluding the cities of refuge?
Answer:
Scripture:

18. Who killed Sisera by driving a tent peg through his head?

Answer:

Scripture:

19. Who ate honey not knowing that his father had cursed anyone who ate before evening?

Answer:

Scripture:

20. What kind of human sacrifice was done by the Ammonites to worship their pagan gods?

Answer:

Scripture:

21. Which king ordered thirty-one men to rescue Jeremiah from a mudhole?

Answer:

Scripture:

22. Who ordered the building of the first fleet of ships recorded in the Bible?

Answer:

Scripture:

23. How many years was King Jehoiachin of Judah kept in prison in Babylon?

Answer:

Scripture:

24. Which king of Judah had his eyes burned out?

Answer:

Scripture

25. What Baal-worshipping queen massacred her own grandchildren?

Answer:

Scripture:

26. Who leaned back on their chair and broke their neck?

Answer:

Scripture:

27. Who was thrown from a high window and devoured by dogs?

Answer:

Scripture:

28. Why did Eli's daughter-in-law name her baby boy Ichabod?

Answer:

Scripture:

29. Whose hair was caught in a tree during battle and was stabbed in the heart with a javelin?

Answer:

Scripture:

30. How many apostles are listed in the New Testament?

Answer:

Scripture:

# NOTES

# FILL IN THE BLANKS

Add the scripture at the end of each.

1. So _____ died, and his_____ _____, and
   all his _____ died together. Scripture_____

2. And the _____ of the _____ continued in
   the_____ of_____ the_____
   three months: and the _____ blessed _____,
   and all his _____. Scripture_____

3. Moreover it is _____ in _____, that a man
   be found _____. Scripture_____

4. For the Lord _____ the _____ of the
   _____ : but the _____ of the_____
   shall _____. Scripture_____

5. For the _____ of a _____ woman drop
   as an _____, and her _____ is smoother
   than _____: But her end is _____ as
   _____, _____ as a _____ _____
   . Scripture_____

6. My _____ shalt thou hear in the _____, O
   Lord; in the _____ will I direct my _____ unto
   thee, and will look _____. Scripture_____

7. For _____ us was the _____ preached, as well as unto _____: but the _____ preached did not _____ them, not being _____ with _____ in them that _____ it. Scripture_____

8. There is _____ _____ nor _____, there is neither _____ nor _____, there is neither _____ nor _____: for ye are _____ _____ in Christ Jesus. Scripture_____

9. And being _____ _____, that what he had _____, he was able also to _____. Scripture_____

10. And she went and did _____ to the saying of _____: and she, and he, and her _____, did eat many _____. Scripture_____

11. When they_____ these things, they were _____ to the _____, and they_____ on him with their _____. Scripture_____

12. My _____ is of God, which _____ the _____ in heart. Scripture_____

13. And there was no _____ for the _____ : and they _____ themselves together against _____ and _____. Scripture_____

14. The _____ shall not _____ for the _____, neither shall the _____ _____ for the _____, but every man shall _____ for his own _____. Scripture_____

15. _____, and _____ unto the Lord your God: Let all that be round about him bring _____ unto him that _____ to be _____. Scripture_____

16. I have _____ out, as a _____ cloud, thy _____, and, as a _____, thy _____ : return unto me, for I have _____ thee. Scripture_____

17. I form the _____, and create _____: I make _____, and create _____: I the Lord do all these _____. Scripture_____

18. A man's _____ shall bring him _____; but _____ shall _____ the _____ in spirit. Scripture_____

19. Let us be _____ and _____, and give _____ to him: for the _____ of the _____ is come and his _____ hath made _____ ready. Scripture_____

20. For we _____ that there are some which _____
    among you _____, _____ not at all, but are
    _____. Scripture_____

21. A _____ reed shall he not _____, and smoking
    _____ shall he not _____, till he send forth
    _____ unto _____. Scripture_____

22. Let the _____ of my _____, and the
    _____ of my _____, be _____
    in thy _____, O Lord, my _____, and my
    _____. Scripture_____

23. As thou hast _____ him _____ over all
    _____, that he should give _____ _____ to as
    many as thou hast _____ him. Scripture_____

24. All that _____ by _____ their _____
    at thee: they _____ and _____ their
    _____ at the _____ of Jerusalem, saying,
    is this the _____ that men call The _____
    of _____, The _____ of the whole earth?
    Scripture_____

25. But _____ is of old like a _____ of water: yet
    they shall _____ away. _____, stand, shall they
    _____: but none shall look back. Scripture_____

26. And the _____ took of their _____, and asked not _____ at the _____ of the _____. Scripture_____

27. But to _____ of the _____ said he at anytime, _____ on my _____ hand, until I make thine _____ thy _____? Scripture_____

28. For _____ if some did not _____? Shall their _____ make the _____ of God _____ effect? Scripture_____

29. In these _____ a great _____ of _____ folk, of _____, halt, _____, waiting for the _____ of the _____. Scripture_____

30. And a great _____ followed him, because they _____ his _____ which he did on them that were _____. Scripture_____

# NOTES

The fear of the Lord is the beginning of knowledge: but fools despise wisdom and instruction. (Proverbs 1:7 KJV)

But God commendeth his Love toward us, in that, while we were yet sinners, Christ died for us. (Romans 5:8 KJV)

If we confess our sins, he is faithful and just to forgive us our sins, and to cleanse us from all unrighteousness. (1 John 1:9 KJV)

But whoso keepeth his word, in him verily is the love of God perfected: hereby know we that we are in him. (1 John 2:5 KJV)

But thou, O Lord, art a shield for me, my glory, and the lifter up of mine head. (Psalm 3:3 KJV)

But he answered and said, It is written, Man shall no live by bread alone, but by every word that proceedeth out of the mouth of God. (Matthew 4:4 KJV)

# Women of the Bible

**Who Am I?**

Match the woman's name with her identity.

1. Jerioth     wife of Uriah
2. Gomer     sister of King Agrippa
3. Phoebe     Jewish prophetess
4. Hephziba    Haran's daughter
5. Taphath     wife and prostitute
6. Elizabeth    prophetess and judge
7. Candace    prophetess and mother of Samuel
8. Lois      wife of Asher
9. Eve      Hosea and Gomer's daughter
10. Martha     one of Job's daughters
11. Anna     Ruth's sister-in-law
12. Judith     first convert to Christianity
13. Zilpah     Mordecai's cousin
14. Shiphrah    wife of Moses
15. Deborah    first wife
16. Orpah     second wife of Caleb
17. Bernice    Solomon's daughter
18. Hadassah    Timothy's grandmother
19. Dinah     wife of King Hezekiah
20. Jedidah    Mary's sister
21. Iscah     deaconess

22. Jemima                Tabitha

23. Lo-Ruhamah     Mahlon and Chilion's mother

24. Zipporah            mother of Josiah

25. Naarah              Ethiopian queen

26. Ephrath            Leah's handmaid

27. Hannah             Hebrew midwife

28. Bathsheba        daughter of Jacob

29. Lydia                wife of Caleb

30. Ruth                 Jesus's cousin

31. Dorcas             wife of Esau

# Notes

# Names of God

**Match the Name with the Meaning**

(You may use other resources)

| | | |
|---|---|---|
| 1. | ELOHIM | the Lord, my righteousness |
| 2. | JEHOVAH | the almighty God |
| 3. | EL ROI | the Lord who sees |
| 4. | EL SHADDAI | the Lord, my provider |
| 5. | EL OLAM | the Lord of host |
| 6. | JEHOVAH JIREH | the most high God |
| 7. | JEHOVAH RAPHA | the Lord, my creator |
| 8. | JEHOVAH NISSI | the Lord, my peace |
| 9. | JEHOVAH MAKADESH | the everlasting God |
| 10. | JEHOVAH TSIDKESH | the Lord, my abiding presence |
| 11. | JEHOVAH SHALOM | the Lord, my master |
| 12. | JEHOVAH ROHI | the Lord, my healer |
| 13. | JEHOVAH SHAMMAH | my Lord God |
| 14. | JEHOVAH SABAOTH | the Lord, my banner |
| 15. | El ELYON | the Lord, my sanctifier |
| 16. | ADONAI | the Lord, my shepherd |
| 17. | ELKANNA | the Lord, my shield |
| 18. | JEHOVAH-UZI | the Lord, my strength |
| 19. | JEHOVAH-HOSHE'AH | the Lord who saves |
| 20. | JEHOVAH MAGEN | jealous God |

# What's Your Thought?

Below is the list of Hebrew months with their corresponding
English month of the year, as taught by my professor.
List your thoughts and findings.
(This is a research section; you can use any resource you desire.)

January _____ Sebat _____

February _____ Adar _____

March _____ Abib or Nisan _____

April _____ Zif _____

May _____ Sivan_____

June _____ Tammuz _____

July _____ Ab _____

August _____ Elul _____

September _____ Ethanim or Tisri _____

October _____ Bul _____

November _____ Chisleu _____

December _____ Tebet _____

# NOTES

# WHAT'S YOUR THOUGHT?

Below is a list of New Testament keywords,
as taught by my professor.
List your thoughts and findings.
(This is a research section; you can use any resource you desire.)

1.  Matthew _____ Kingdom _____
2.  Mark _____ Immediately _____
3.  Luke _____ Savior _____
4.  John _____ Believe _____
5.  Acts _____ Conversion _____
6.  Romans_____ Righteousness_____
7.  1 Corinthians _____ Problems _____
8.  2 Corinthians _____ Comfort _____
9.  Galatians_____ Liberty _____
10. Ephesians _____ The Church _____
11. Philippians _____ Joy _____
12. Colossians _____ Fullness _____
13. 1 Thessalonians _____ Hope _____
14. 2 Thessalonians_____ The Day of the Lord_____
15. 1 Timothy _____ Minister _____
16. 2 Timothy _____ Preach _____
17. Titus _____ Sober _____
18. Philemon _____ Receive _____
19. Hebrews _____ Better _____
20. James _____ Practical _____

21. 1 Peter _____ Suffering _____

22. 2 Peter_____ Knowledge _____

23. 1 John _____ Fellowship _____

24. 2 John_____ Doctrine _____

25. 3 John_____ Truth _____

26. Jude _____ Contend _____

27. Revelation _____ Overcome _____

# NOTES

For I know the thoughts that I think toward you, saith the Lord, thoughts of peace, and not of evil, to give you an expected end. (Jeremiah 29:11 KJV)

For my thoughts are not your thoughts, neither are your ways my ways, saith the Lord. (Isaiah 55:8 KJV)

How precious also are thy thoughts unto me, O God! How great is the sum of them! (Psalm 139:17 KJV)

Let everything that hath breath praise the LORD. Praise ye the LORD. (Psalm 150:6 KJV)

Stand fast therefore in the liberty wherewith Christ hath made us free, and be not entangled again with the yoke of bondage. (Galatians 5:1 KJV)

SHIRLEY D. GARRETT

# WHAT'S IN A NAME?

Match each woman's name with how she is known.

1.  Eve                         woman of discard
2.  Lydia                       woman of transformation
3.  Elisabeth                   woman of patience
4.  The Shunammite              woman of bravely
5.  Ruth                        woman of patriotism
6.  Miriam                      woman of faith
7.  Martha                      woman of promise
8.  Esther                      woman of business
9.  Abigail                     woman of prayer
10. Hagar                       woman of curiosity
11. Deborah                     woman of generosity
12. The Syrophenician           woman of grace
13. Mary Magdalene              woman of hospitality
14. The Widow                   woman of capability
15. Rachel                      woman of worry
16. Hannah                      woman of humility
17. Sarah                       woman of ambition
18. Priscilla                   woman of self-sacrificing
19. Jehosheba                   woman of persistence
20. Joanna                      woman of constancy

# NOTES

# How Did They Die?

Match the name with how each person died.

| | | |
|---|---|---|
| 1. | Absalom | old age |
| 2. | Eli | eaten by worms |
| 3. | Enoch | tent peg hammer through head |
| 4. | John the Baptist | fell from a third-story window |
| 5. | Eglon | millstone shattered his skull |
| 6. | Sisera | gave up the ghost |
| 7. | James | cut into twelve pieces |
| 8. | Saul | leaned back in chair and broke neck |
| 9. | Eutychus | javelin through the heart |
| 10. | Abraham | head served on a platter |
| 11. | Ananias | stoned to death |
| 12. | Methuselah | thrown from a high window |
| 13. | Lot's wife | a lie |
| 14. | King Agrippa | beheaded |
| 15. | Abimelech | hung himself |
| 16. | Levite concubine | fell on his own sword |
| 17. | Jezebel | carried away to heaven |
| 18. | Judas | stabbed while on the toilet |
| 19. | Stephen | turned into a pillar of salt |
| 20. | Moses | placed in a crack in the mountain |

# NOTES

# FIND THE WORDS

Using the twenty letters below, find twenty-five words from
Psalm 1
(Letters can be used more than once, and
there are no three-letter words.)

## RCFLY
## UIHDV
## TOSKE
## GNPWA

Answer worksheet

1. _____
2. _____
3. _____
4. _____
5. _____
6. _____
7. _____
8. _____
9. _____
10. _____
11. _____
12. _____

13. _____
14. _____
15. _____
16. _____
17. _____
18. _____
19. _____
20. _____
21. _____
22. _____
23. _____
24. _____
25. _____

# Find the Word

Using the twenty letters below, find twenty words from
The Ten Commandments (Exodus 20:3–17)
(Letters can be used more than once, and
there are no three-letter words.)

## VLSAG

## CYROI

## EMTDF

## BWUNH

Answer worksheet

1. _____
2. _____
3. _____
4. _____
5. _____
6. _____
7. _____
8. _____
9. _____
10. _____
11. _____
12. _____

13. _____

14. _____

15. _____

16. _____

17. _____

18. _____

19. _____

20. _____

Shirley D. Garrett

# FIND THE WORDS

Using the twenty letters below, find twenty words from
The Lord's Prayer (Matthew 6:9–13)
(Letters can be used more than once, and
there are no three-letter words.)

## WDFLR
## PMSKI
## NTEVB
## HYOGA

Answer worksheet

1. _____
2. _____
3. _____
4. _____
5. _____
6. _____
7. _____
8. _____
9. _____
10. _____
11. _____
12. _____

13. _____

14. _____

15. _____

16. _____

17. _____

18. _____

19. _____

20. _____

# TRUE OR FALSE

1.  Methuselah was the oldest living person in the bible but died before his father. T or F:_____ Scripture:_____

2.  Abram was ninety-nine years old when God changed his name to Abraham. T or F:____ Scripture:_____

3.  Rebekah and Tamar both had twins. T or F:_____ Scripture:_____

4.  Paul had had his "thorn in the flesh" for fifteen years when he wrote 2 Corinthians 12. T or F:_____ Scripture:_____

5.  There are three books in the Bible named after women. T or F:_____ Scripture:_____

6.  The king of Judah's feet became diseased during his old age. T or F:____ Scripture:_____

7.  The disciple Thomas was also known as Didymus. T or F:____ Scripture:_____

8.  Daniel abstained from eating the king's rich food for fourteen days. T or F:____ Scripture:_____

9.  Jeremiah lived in a town called Uz. T or F:____ Scripture:_____

10. The raven brought Elijah food three times a day. T or F:____ Scripture:_____

11. The locusts were allowed to torture humankind for one year in Revelation. T or F:____ Scripture:_____

12. Absalom had a daughter and a sister named Tamar. T or F:____ Scripture:_____

13. Paul was shipwrecked on the Red Sea. T or F:_____ Scripture:_____

14. Lapidoth was the husband of the first female Israelite leader. T or F:____ Scripture:_____

15. Hannah made a coat for her son every year. T or F:_____ Scripture:_____

16. Abraham's second wife gave him six children. T or F:_____ Scripture:_____

17. David was offered anything he wanted by God. T or F:_____ Scripture:_____

18. Philip had a vision of a man asking him to come to Macedonia. T or F:_____ Scripture:_____

19. All four Gospels record the miracle of feeding the five thousand. T or F:_____ Scripture:_____

20. God gave Job ten children to replace his ten children who died. T or F:____ Scripture:_____

# NOTES

# Word Search Puzzles

## Find the Word in the Puzzle

Words can go in any direction. Words can share
letters as they cross over each other.

## The Runaway Slave

```
B Q T C L E U P P W I L L I N G L Y O S
Q E O Z O P H R E C E I V E H I T E N R
J V L W F I C O N V E N I E N T O C E E
I E E O L D D F K B W P R T M X X N S Y
Z S N E V E E D A D I C E R C Q X E I A
T S M D G E J E H P P H F G G V N I M R
D O E N Q X D X C Y D F R Q U T L D U P
N L O P L E N X P N E G E E S U A E S A
W R M R E H T O R B E T S M A A Z B X Q
W E X M A A X M I C X D H P D G L O C U
G E R E Z J K D D V Q I I F P C T U W T
Y R E C L F I I T Y V Q C F O U H U T Y
F N N G H B N J C D T J A K N C Z R G E
U C O H R B A U B C V E I T R O L B C W
M X S Y X B B T H F C I S U R C C K E O
J Z I N X A W M I O Z Q H W G Y A U O I
T G R S M A A F J F M C D A E T S X F M
P H P Q P R L H V A O H K D Z W T E Q Q
S W Z G E R K G C K A R F J W Q O H S B
T A S Q T I C E C J W Y P X H B O U J F
```

| | | | |
|---|---|---|---|
| PRISONER | WILLINGLY | WRONGED | PHILEMON |
| PAUL | NECESSITY | CONVENIENT | STEAD |
| RECEIVE | BELOVED | CHURCH | CONFIDENCE |
| SALUTE | REFRESH | OBEDIENCE | BROTHER |
| ONESIMUS | OWEST | PRAYERS | PROFITABLE |

# TWO

# Prominent Women of the Bible

```
A  K  W  B  Q  M  W  B  Q  H  C  C  W  Y  F  T  K  A  R  B
C  V  I  J  O  Z  F  T  O  T  A  L  T  R  U  M  N  A  Z  A
L  Z  M  L  W  V  A  U  T  X  Z  K  W  I  H  L  C  M  O  H
D  Z  R  K  Q  A  E  P  O  A  T  N  E  A  V  H  H  T  J  A
T  E  P  J  T  Z  B  H  H  I  E  N  R  B  E  W  E  Q  G  R
J  Y  B  L  D  V  D  T  O  Z  F  A  T  L  E  R  L  M  L  L
Y  D  L  O  A  M  E  M  G  N  S  T  D  M  B  R  Y  I  M  P
L  B  I  V  R  B  Y  Y  A  D  I  S  T  D  L  L  Y  R  V  E
H  T  U  R  A  A  B  E  H  S  F  O  N  E  E  U  Q  I  N  F
L  O  W  S  P  F  H  O  I  U  G  D  Y  A  K  Y  C  A  X  W
E  Z  I  U  R  E  V  R  X  M  O  T  Q  I  Z  C  D  M  F  N
Q  L  B  B  U  C  U  E  E  Y  O  A  P  T  G  E  L  O  X  H
E  C  U  I  B  A  J  N  L  F  Y  A  V  H  E  V  E  L  A  Z
D  O  R  C  A  S  E  M  I  E  J  O  N  S  X  O  C  N  V  E
M  I  P  Y  Y  O  Z  O  E  C  A  J  C  A  J  C  N  T  J  V
A  H  T  R  A  M  E  Q  S  B  E  H  M  V  V  A  O  H  W  C
N  H  Z  O  X  L  B  R  T  X  Z  A  V  I  H  W  R  J  T  O
H  X  P  L  F  J  E  C  H  X  R  F  P  L  B  A  P  C  G  X
H  O  P  R  J  R  L  U  E  Y  M  Y  Y  S  Q  S  J  Q  I  B
G  O  E  B  D  X  A  B  R  P  K  L  F  H  W  V  W  G  J  V
```

| | | | |
|---|---|---|---|
| MARY | REBEKAH | SARAH | VASHTI |
| RUTH | EUNICE | QUEENOFSHEBA | DORCAS |
| ESTHER | RAHAB | HANNAH | RACHEL |
| JEZEBEL | LEAH | MIRIAM | DEBORAH |
| NAOMI | ELISABETH | EVE | MARTHA |

SHIRLEY D. GARRETT

# The Red Sea

```
L V B S X R Z B I A P B H L B N V B Z G
L E O Z M O S E S G F E F T B O K N I D
M Y G V L Z B J R U C B N I E I T X P K
B X N N W Q B W A W Q S Z C G T F N R Z
D A N G A A V F E B G X W B D A H K K S
X S N V D S T M L R V L E W K V J G A X
X R O G W C R E J P X M R H C L D L I O
G R O U N D H P R A E S H F V A Y B L F
L O M W I P G S H S E A T A E S T I Z A
P U R S U E D Y V A T J R B B A N U T D
K H I O V A D X O Z R C E R N E R C C U
K Z A L Y N U L O S O A V T M Z X E R O
S T O I R A H C N S D K O E Z S W S D L
J G G L J Q X A O Y Z U S H T J X A A C
L L B S Z O I U E D J R Y R E L Q M C G
W U B X A T Z A V U O W E C X D Y T L S
M I Z D P N D G W H K T S C P J X Y C L
P O N Y I H O U I J C D F M Z C Y X Q C
V I G E N D C P D H O F B P I E J P I Y
W E L C X E W C I B Y A I D Z R M I P T
```

| | | | |
|---|---|---|---|
| SALVATION | GROUND | EGYPTIANS | WATERS |
| MOSES | ROD | PHARAOH | GOD |
| ISRAEL | SEA | STRETCH | FIGHTETH |
| CHARIOTS | FEARED | ANGEL | OVERTHREW |
| CLOUD | HORSEMEN | WIND | PURSUED |

# The Last Supper

```
H E N T A U Q C D M S L J P N R K Q R V
E H J Y L F D A N O O Y K S R E D R H V
J M H L P F U G M R R D N F F T N Q U T
P B N E O X G R Y G R H G D J S F G G P
B E T R A Y E D H T O S H N B A P A O O
P G F X P H K A W U W Z A H I M Q I U J
W Z T R W G E E N M F L W Y Z K X F L B
P K U E B M L L L C U A B B L O O D Y B
N C R U S V E K W A L Q A H A N N I Z L
E K U E E A N O I S S I M E R Y D U D E
H B C X V P C B E C I W C A O P D A T S
C E E E S O S Z Y P O L X C W A E O M S
Y K N B L P S R X W P K U K H R R W B E
D E F C J K H S D Z U A S G B B B R K D
D G X U E T P W A R C D C E P L E D Q Y
G O D Z E F S E L P I C S I D K L K D E
F A M P N Q O B U J T N H M T S A E F K
S B P O W S I R Q E P L K Y C F B N C T
Y I U F G C X G T L H Y K F R V B U N Z
D O D Q D K X Y C H B R I T I K G N Z U
```

| | | | |
|---|---|---|---|
| UNLEAVENED | KINGDOM | CUP | DRINK |
| DISCIPLES | HYMN | JUDAS | PASSOVER |
| BODY | BREAD | FEAST | TWELVE |
| MASTER | BLOOD | REMISSION | DIPPETH |
| BETRAYED | BLESSED | SORROWFUL | HENCEFORTH |

SHIRLEY D. GARRETT

# The First Passover

```
H L S M B A H S U E S R E Z O S W S O Y
Z F N I J M G E Q F E M Q F E C I A M A
O X E N A E W L Q O L I E V D K D K W S
B D G S C R V C N A P T O L R B K B N B
E G R U O C S A F D I D H K A P E F B A
E T V W F H A R I P C G G U K S A B X I
G N H P H A Z I Y V S H E E P T U X M P
E V O R D N P M X T I C Z O H C X R V X
X I Q C L D L Z D M D M X E C Y I X E L
X V N H V I S V Z S O E R W V K S R Q J
R S H E U S I Z U N L U D Y H T Y I Q K
W J C Z S E R S E Y P T P J F D T W X Y
Z S B R N I E Y D D L E J A Z X R C G F
Y F C F I J R O C Q Z M O C S F O Y P J
D O R P N P B T P J Q P Z Y S S F R E Q
J O R Z Q C T Q R R Q L H M M H O Y W H
B W N T E A W U J I I E P A Y F X V M U
I O B D S H E K R E P O Y G A H N M E J
V R B R F E A S T E R R R B R M P D T R
H S C L E T D V K H A U Q L T X V J K B
```

| | | | |
|---|---|---|---|
| PASSOVER | SCRIPTURE | DISCIPLES | DESTROY |
| JERUSALEM | RISEN | DROVE | TEMPLE |
| MIRACLES | FORTYSIX | FATHER | BODY |
| JESUS | DOVES | SCOURGE | MONEY |
| SHEEP | OXEN | FEAST | MERCHANDISE |

# Men of the Bible

```
O F P P G K M P B V L P L D T W N V F T
V T X F S I N R N V F S G M Z F N C Q M
X I P L Y G E L I Z T O P A V T N H T Z
F N K A B R A H A M R N O K L O I N A T
L E I N A D C X S Y N B T M M K E V N I
J E S U S A R X G Y H D S O A H Z D N M
Q Z J I L K Q E C U O C L B E T I X I O
J U W E U M Y X T N J O C M N V T R A T
S A B H D O L P N E S D I C A U C H C H
A R C S S S U Y B W P A C D B V H S E Y
M X W O Q E A V J M H E L I J A H N I W
U N M B B S P F H R N V V H W P I W M N
E M D T R Q G I W I S Y X X U L L J N E
L X Q Z I J W Q K V I X Y E M V N W P Z
J W O X O W Z R N J P O B Y R N Y D V Q
H O H E S R P T O O K R A M L U A S D H
H A S N J K U B H Z E K I D C E H I I A
F U O E X M E X B H X D O M A D A I I U
Y S H N P K V N F M W G I F L S Q S G Z
C E D X W H K J M Z N Z Z G T M H K M R
```

| | | | | |
|---|---|---|---|---|
| ADAM | NOAH | MARK | NEHEMIAH | TIMOTHY |
| JOHN | SOLOMON | CAIN | PETER | MATTHEW |
| ABRAHAM | JACOB | ELIJAH | DAVID | JOSEPH |
| MOSES | CALEB | SAMUEL | JOB | JESUS |
| DANIEL | GIDEON | SAUL | BOAZ | PAUL |

SHIRLEY D. GARRETT

# ANSWERS

**Search the Scriptures**

1. What did Jacob name the place where he wrestled with the angel (God)?
   a. Peniel
   b. Genesis 32:30

2. Who almost lost his life bringing money to Paul in prison in Rome?
   a. Epaphroditus
   b. Philippians 2:25–30

3. To which tribe of Israel did Paul belong?
   a. Benjamin
   b. Philippians 3:5

4. Who died during childbirth after praying for a second son?
   a. Rachel
   b. Genesis 35:16–19

5. In whose house did the Ark of God remain for three months?
   a. Obed-edom
   b. 1 Chronicles 13:14

6. When the anger of the Lord was hot against Israel, to which king did he sell them?

a. Chushanrishathaim

b. Judges 3:8

7. Which book of the New Testament mentions the second coming of Christ in every chapter?

a. 1 Thessalonians

8. Who used sorcery to bewitch the people of Samaria, but after hearing Philip preach Christ was baptized, he continued with Philip?

a. Simon

b. Acts 8:11–13

9. At whose house did the gentiles first receive the Holy Ghost and speak with tongues that magnified God?

a. Cornelius's house

b. Acts 10:44–46

10. Which apostle died in exile and was the only apostle not to suffer martyrdom?

a. The apostle John

b. John 21:20–23

11. In which city did God slaughter 50,070 men because they looked into the Ark of the Covenant?

a. Bethshemesh

b. 1 Samuel 6:19

12. For which of David's actions did God cause a plague on Israel?

    a. Counting the soldiers

    b. 2 Samuel 24:1–15

13. What animal killed forty-two children who ridiculed the bald head of the prophet Elisha?

    a. Bear

    b. 2 Kings 2:23–24

14. How did God designate those who would be spared in the Jerusalem massacre prophesied by Ezekiel?

    a. By a mark on the forehead

    b. Ezekiel 9:4

15. What request did Jephthah's daughter make before allowing herself to be sacrificed?

    a. To go to the hills for two (2) months and roam and be with her friends.

    b. Judges 11:37

16. Which prominent individual was the first to be cremated in the Bible?

    a. Saul

    b. 1 Samuel 13:12

17. How many cities in Canaan were given to the Levites, excluding the cities of refuge?

    a. Forty-two

    b. Numbers 35:6–7

18. Who killed Sisera by driving a tent peg through his head?
    a. Jael
    b. Judges 4:21

19. Who ate honey not knowing that his father had cursed anyone who ate before evening?
    a. Jonathan
    b. 1 Samuel 14:24–27

20. What kind of human sacrifice was done by the Ammonites to worship their pagan gods?
    a. Burning little children
    b. Leviticus 18:21

21. Which king ordered thirty-one men to rescue Jeremiah from a mudhole?
    a. Zedekiah
    b. Jeremiah 38:1–10

22. Who ordered the building of the first fleet of ships recorded in the Bible?
    a. Solomon
    b. 1 Kings 9:26

23. How many years was King Jehoiachin of Judah kept in prison in Babylon?
    a. Thirty-seven
    b. Jeremiah 52:31

24. Which king of Judah had his eyes burned out?
    a.  Athaliah
    b.  2 kings 11:1–2

25. What Baal-worshiping queen massacred her own grandchildren?
    a.  Athaliah
    b.  2 Kings 11:1–2

26. Who leaned back on his chair and broke his neck?
    a.  Eli
    b.  1 Samuel 4:1

27. Who was thrown from a high window and devoured by dogs?
    a.  Jezebel
    b.  2 Kings 9:30–37

28. Why did Eli's daughter-in-law name her baby boy Ichabod?
    a.  The name meant, "The glory has departed from Israel."
    b.  1 Samuel 4:21

29. Whose hair was caught in a tree during battle and was stabbed in the heart with a javelin?
    a.  Absalom
    b.  2 Samuel 18:9–15

30. How many apostles are listed in the New Testament?
    a.  fourteen
    b.  Original twelve plus Mattias (Judas's replacement) and Paul

# Fill in the Blank

1. So **Saul** died, and his **three sons**, and all his **house** died together. Scripture: 1 Chronicles 10:6

2. And the **ark** of the **Lord** continued in the **house** of **Obed-edom** the **Glittite** three months: and the **Lord** blessed **Obed-edom**, and all his **household**. Scripture: 2 Samuel 6:11

3. Moreover it is **required** in **stewards**, that a man be found **faithful**. Scripture: 1 Corinthians 4:2

4. For the Lord **knoweth** the **way** of the **righteous**: but the **way** of the **ungodly** shall **perish**. Scripture: Psalm 1:6

5. For the **lips** of a **strange** woman drop as an **honeycomb**, and her **mouth** is smoother than **oil**: But her end is **bitter** as **wormwood**, **sharp** as a **two edged sword**. Scripture: Proverbs 5:3–4

6. My **voice** shalt thou hear in the **morning**, O Lord; in the **morning** will I direct my **prayer** unto thee, and will look **up**. Scripture: Psalm 5:3

7. For **unto** us was the **gospel** preached, as well as unto **them**: but the **word** preached did not **profit** them, not being **mixed** with **faith** in them that **heard** it. Scripture: Hebrews 4:2

8. There is **neither Jew** nor **Greek**, there is neither **bond** nor **free**, there is neither **male** nor **female**: for ye are **all one** in Christ Jesus. Scripture: Galatians 3:28

9. And being **fully persuaded** that, what he had **promised**, he was able also to **perform**. Scripture: Romans 4:21

10. And she went and did **according** to the saying of **Elijah**: and she, and he, and her **house**, did eat many **days**. Scripture: 1 Kings 17:15

11. When they **heard** these things, they were **cut** to the **heart**, and they **gnashed** on him with their **teeth**. Scripture: Acts 7:54

12. My **defence** is of God, which **saveth** the **upright** in heart. Scripture: Psalm 7:10

13. And there was no **water** for the **congregation**: and they **gathered** themselves together against **Moses** and **Aaron**. Scripture: Numbers 20:2

14. The **fathers** shall not **die** for the **children**, neither shall the **children die** for the **fathers**, but every man shall **die** for his own **sin**. Scripture: 2 Chronicles 25:4b

15. **Vow**, and **pay** unto the Lord your God: Let all that be round about him bring **presents** unto him that **ought** to be **feared**. Scripture: Psalm 76:11

16. I have **blotted** out, as a **thick** cloud, thy **transgressions**, and, as a **cloud**, thy **sins**: return unto me, for I have **redeemed** thee. Scripture: Isaiah 44:22

17. I form the **light**, and create **darkness**: I make **peace**, and create **evil**: I the Lord do all these **things**. Scripture: Isaiah 45:7

18. A man's **pride** shall bring him **low**; but **honour** shall **uphold** the **humble** in spirit. Scripture: Proverbs 29:23

19. Let us be **glad** and **rejoice**, and give **honour** to him: for the **marriage** of the **Lamb** is come and his **wife** hath made **herself** ready. Scripture: Revelation 19:7

20. For we **hear** that there are some which **walk** among you **disorderly**, **working** not at all, but are **busybodies**. Scripture: 2 Thessalonians 3:11

21. A **bruised** reed shall he not **break**, and smoking **flax** shall he not **quench**, till he send forth **judgment** unto **victory**. Scripture: Matthew 12:20

22. Let the **words** of my **mouth**, and the **meditation** of my **heart**, be **acceptable** in thy **sight**, O Lord, my **strength**, and my **redeemer**. Scripture: Psalm 19:14

23. As thou hast **given** him **power** over all **flesh**, that he should give **eternal life** to as many as thou hast **given** him. Scripture: John 17:2

24. All that **pass** by **clap** their **hands** at thee: they **hiss** and **wag** their **head** at the **daughter** of Jerusalem, saying, is this the **city** that men call The **perfection** of **beauty**, The **joy** of the whole earth? Scripture: Lamentations 2:15

25. But **Nineveh** is of old like a **pool** of water: yet they shall **flee** away. **Stand**, stand, shall they **cry**: but none shall look back. Scripture: Nahum 2:8

26. And the **men** took of their **victuals**, and asked not **counsel** at the **mouth** of the **Lord**. Scripture: Joshua 9:14

27. But to **which** of the **angels** said he at anytime, **Sit** on my **right** hand, until I make thine **enemies** thy **footstool**? Scripture: Hebrews 1:13

28. For **what** if some did not **believe**? Shall their **unbelief** make the **faith** of God **without** effect? Scripture: Romans 3:3

29. In these **lay** a great **multitude** of **impotent** folk, of **blind**, halt, **withered**, waiting for the **moving** of the **water**. Scripture: John 5:3

30. And a great **multitude** followed him, because they **saw** his **miracles** which he did on them that were **diseased**. Scripture: John 6:2

# MATCH THE WOMAN'S NAME WITH HER IDENTITY

1. Jerioth—wife of Caleb
2. Gomer—wife and prostitute
3. Phoebe—deaconess
4. Hephzibah—wife of King Hezekiah
5. Taphath—Solomon's daughter
6. Elizabeth—Jesus's cousin
7. Candace—Ethiopian queen
8. Lois—Timothy's grandmother
9. Eve—first wife
10. Martha—Mary's sister
11. Anna—Jewish prophetess
12. Judith—wife of Esau
13. Zilpah—Leah's handmaid
14. Shiphrah—Hebrew midwife
15. Deborah—prophetess and judge
16. Orpah—Ruth's sister-in-law
17. Bernice—sister of King Agrippa
18. Hadassah—Mordecai's cousin
19. Dinah—daughter of Jacob
20. Jedidah—mother of Josiah
21. Iscah—Haran's daughter
22. Jemima—one of Job's daughters
23. Lo-Ruhamah—Hosea and Gomer's daughter
24. Zipporah—wife of Moses

25. Naarah—wife of Asher
26. Ephrat—second wife of Caleb
27. Hannah—prophetess and mother of Samuel
28. Bathsheba—wife of Uriah
29. Lydia—first woman to convert to Christianity
30. Naomi—Mahlon and Chilion's mother
31. Dorcus—Tabitha

# NAMES OF GOD

1. EL OHIM—God of power and might
2. JEHOVAH—the Lord
3. EL ROI—the Lord who sees
4. EL SHADDAI—the almighty God
5. EL OLAM—the everlasting God
6. JEHOVAH JIREH—the Lord, my provider
7. JEHOVAH RAPHA—the Lord, my healer
8. JEHOVAH NISSI—the Lord, my banner
9. JEHOVAH MAKADESH—the Lord who sanctifies
10. JEHOVAH TSIDKESH—the Lord, our righteousness
11. JEHOVAH SHALOM—the Lord, my peace
12. JEHOVAH ROHI—the Lord, my shepherd
13. JEHOVAH SHAMMAH—the Lord, my abiding presence
14. JEHOVAH SABAOTH—the Lord of hosts
15. EL ELYON—the most high God
16. ADONAI—the Lord, my master
17. EL KANNA—jealous God
18. JEHOVAH-UZI—the Lord, my strength
19. JEHOVAH-HOSHE'AH—the Lord, my creator
20. JEHOVAH MAGEN—the Lord, my shield

# WHAT'S IN A NAME?

1.  Woman of curiosity
2.  Woman of business
3.  Woman of humility
4.  Woman of hospitality
5.  Woman of constancy
6.  Woman of ambition
7.  Woman of worry
8.  Woman of sacrifice
9.  Woman of capability
10. Woman of discard
11. Woman of patriotism
12. Woman of faith
13. Woman of transformation
14. Woman of persistence
15. Woman of patience
16. Woman of prayer
17. Woman of promise
18. Woman of generosity
19. Woman of bravery
20. Woman of grace

# How Did They Die?

1. Javelin through the heart
2. Leaned back in a chair and broke his neck
3. Carried away to heaven
4. Beheaded, head served on a platter
5. Stabbed while on the toilet
6. Tent peg hammer through the head
7. Crucified upside down
8. Fell on his own sword
9. Fell from three-story window
10. Gave up the ghost
11. A lie
12. Old age
13. Pillar of salt
14. Eaten by worms
15. Millstone shattered his skull
16. Cut in twelve pieces
17. Thrown from a high window
18. Hung himself
19. Stoned to death
20. Placed in a crack in the mountain

# PSALM 1: 1–6

Blessed is the man that **walketh** not in the counsel of the **ungodly**, nor **standeth** in the way of **sinners**, nor sitteth in the **seat** of the **scornful**. But his delight is in the law of the **LORD**, and in his law doth he meditate day and **night**. And he **shall** be like a **tree planted** by the **rivers** of **water**, that bringeth forth his **fruit** in his season; his **leaf** also shall not **wither** and whatsoever he **doeth** shall **prosper**. The ungodly are not so: but are like the **chaff** which the **wind driveth** away. Therefore the ungodly shall not **stand** in the judgment, nor sinners in the congregation of the **righteous**. For the LORD **knoweth** the way of the righteous: but the way of the ungodly shall **perish**.

# The Ten Commandments

Exodus 20:3–17

³ Thou **shalt** have no other gods before me.⁴ Thou shalt not make unto thee any **graven image**, or any likeness of any thing that is in **heaven** above, or that is in the earth beneath, or that is in the water under the **earth**.⁵ Thou shalt not bow down thyself to them, nor serve them: for I the Lord thy God am a jealous God, visiting the iniquity of the fathers upon the children unto the third and fourth generation of them that hate me;⁶ And shewing mercy unto thousands of them that love me, and keep my **commandments**.⁷ **Thou** shalt not take the name of the Lord thy God in vain; for the Lord will not hold him guiltless that taketh his name in **vain**.⁸ **Remember** the sabbath day, to keep it holy.⁹ Six days shalt thou labour, and do all thy work:¹⁰ But the seventh day is the **sabbath** of the Lord thy God: in it thou shalt not do any work, thou, nor thy son, nor thy daughter, thy manservant, nor thy maidservant, nor thy cattle, nor thy stranger that is within thy gates:¹¹ For in six days the Lord made heaven and earth, the sea, and all that in them is, and rested the seventh day: wherefore the Lord blessed the sabbath day, and hallowed it.¹² **Honour** thy **father** and thy **mother**: that thy days may be long upon the land which the Lord thy **God** giveth thee.¹³ Thou shalt not kill.¹⁴ Thou

shalt not **commit adultery**.[15] Thou shalt not **steal**.[16] Thou shalt not bear **false** witness against thy **neighbour**.[17] Thou shalt not **covet** thy neighbour's house, thou shalt not covet thy neighbour's wife, nor his manservant, nor his maidservant, nor his ox, nor his ass, nor any thing that is thy neighbour's.

SHIRLEY D. GARRETT

# THE LORD'S PRAYER

Matthew 6:9–18

[9] After **this** manner therefore pray ye: Our Father which art in **heaven, Hallowed** be thy **name**. [10] Thy **kingdom** come, Thy will be done in **earth**, as it is in heaven. [11] Give us this day our **daily bread**. [12] And forgive us our **debts**, as we **forgive** our debtors. [13] And **lead** us not into temptation, but **deliver** us from **evil**: For thine is the kingdom, and the **power**, and the **glory**, for **ever. Amen**. [14] For if ye forgive men their trespasses, your heavenly **Father** will also forgive you: [15] But if ye forgive not men their **trespasses**, neither will your Father forgive your trespasses. [16] Moreover when ye **fast**, be not, as the hypocrites, of a sad countenance: for they disfigure their faces, that they may appear unto men to fast. Verily I say unto you, They have their reward. [17] But thou, when thou fastest, anoint thine head, and wash thy face; [18] That thou appear not unto men to fast, but unto thy Father which is in secret: and thy Father, which seeth in secret, shall reward thee openly.

# TRUE OR FALSE

1. (T) Enoch his father was carried away to heaven. Genesis 5:24
2. (T) Genesis 17:1–5
3. (T) Genesis 25:24–26, 38:27–30
4. (F) Fourteen years. 2 Corinthians 12
5. (F) Ruth and Esther
6. (T) 1 Kings 15:23
7. (T) John 20:24
8. (F) Ten days. Daniel 1:12
9. (F) Job 1:1
10. (F) Twice a day. 1 Kings 17:6
11. (F) Five Months. Revelation 9:3–5
12. (T) 2 Samuel 13:1–32, 14:27
13. (F) Adriatic Sea. Acts 27:26, 44
14. (T) Judges 4:4
15. (T) 1 Samuel 2:19
16. (T) Genesis 25:1–2
17. (F) Solomon. 1 Kings 3:5
18. (F) Paul. Acts 16:6–10
19. (T) Matthew 14:15–21, Mark 6:35–44, Luke 9:10:17, John 6:1–14
20. (T) Job 42:13

# WORD SEARCH

## The Runaway Slave

# Prominent Women of the Bible

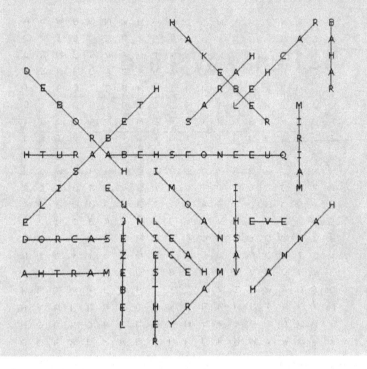

SHIRLEY D. GARRETT

# The Red Sea

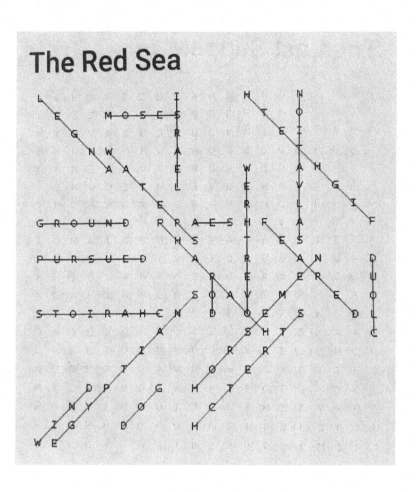

# The Last Supper

SHIRLEY D. GARRETT

# The First Passover

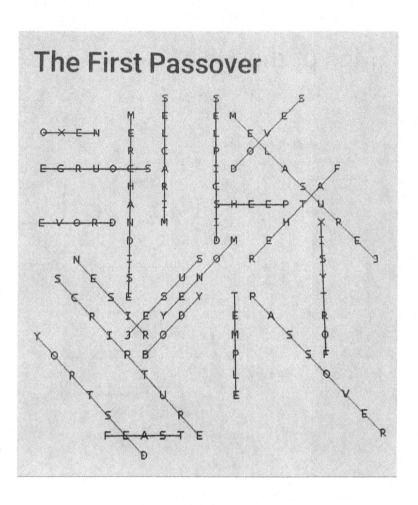

# Men of the Bible

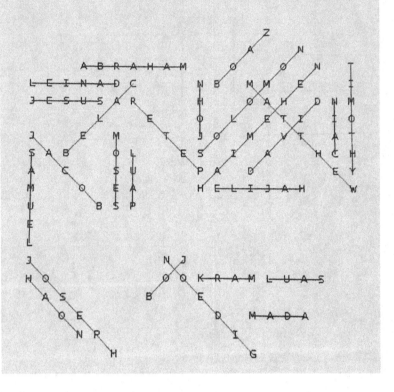

SHIRLEY D. GARRETT

**Congratulations on Completing**

*Search the Scriptures* **Volume 1**

It has been my pleasure to share the scriptures with you. I pray you have been encouraged and motivated to continue to study the word of God. Second Timothy 2:15 says; "Study to shew thyself approved unto God, a workman that needeth not to be ashamed, rightly dividing the word of truth. For I am not ashamed of the gospel of Christ: for it is the power of God unto salvation to everyone that beliveth, to the Jew first, and the Greek."

Fortherein is the righteousness of God revealed from faith to faith: as it is written, The just shall live by faith. (Romans 1:16–17)

So then faith cometh by hearing, and hearing by the word of God. (Romans 10:17)

I pray the LORD bless thee, and keep thee: The LORD make his face shine upon thee, and be gracious unto thee: The LORD lift up his countenance upon thee, and give thee peace. (Numbers 6:24–26)

Now the God of peace, that brought again from the dead our Lord Jesus, that great shepherd of the sheep, through the blood of the everlasting covenant, make you perfect in every good work to do his will, working in you that which is wellpleasing in his sight, through Jesus Christ, to whom be glory forever and ever. Amen. (Hebrews 13:20–21)

God bless,
Shirley D. Garrett

Printed in the United States
by Baker & Taylor Publisher Services